Susan Bregin

THINK LIKE A MAN,
ACT LIKE A LADY,
WORK LIKE A DOG

THINK
LIKE A MAN
ACT
LIKE A LADY
WORK
LIKE A DOG

by Derek A. Newton

Doubleday & Company, Inc., Garden City, New York, 1979

ISBN: 0-385-14691-4
Library of Congress Catalog Card Number 78-14688

To Mum

ACKNOWLEDGMENTS

Someday I would like to write a book and take all the credit for it myself. But this book is certainly *not* the one. Many people have given me inspiration, encouragement, and help. A partial list follows:

THE PIONEERS: Rita Cowles, Betty Dickow, and Joan Wright.

THE PROFESSIONALS: Susan Clifford, Sara Finnegan, Mary Louise Hatten, Rosemary Kaut, Sharon Mc-Gavin, Ann Robinson, Patricia Sides, and Kitty Smiley.

THE NEW BREED: Lawton Fitt, Susan Frederick, Joy Hoffacker, Tory Kerewich, Charlene LeGrand, Davey Levin, Teri Louden, Kathy Martin, Kathy Perry, Patricia Robinson, Mary Anne Townes, Mary Woodford, and Kris Wright.

THE MEN: Dan Burke, Ev Meade, Fred Morton, and John Snook.

THE SCHOLARS: Margaret Hennig and Anne Jardim.

THE COLLEAGUES: Diana Harrington and Eleanor May.

THE SECRETARY: Marie Ball.

The time ain't far off when a
woman won't know any more than
a man.

—Will Rogers

THINK LIKE A MAN,
ACT LIKE A LADY,
WORK LIKE A DOG

INTRODUCTION

The suggestions presented below are for the woman who aspires to a position of major responsibility in an organization and who expects to spend her career working with, working for, and managing men as well as other women. These ideas will probably have little relevance to a woman who seeks only to hold down a good job.

I hope these suggestions provoke thought and discussion. I expect a number of readers to disagree with some of them. After all, I am neither a manager nor a woman, although I have been the former. These ideas flow from my experience in working with and managing women in a business organization, from talking with scores of managerial women, and from having been very closely associated with a successful woman executive from the day I was born.

Some readers will object to my dogmatic style and conservative tone. But younger women, in particular, need to become more aware of how older men think women in business ought to behave. Not only do older men make most of the rules, they determine who gets to play. Your attitudes and behavior may inspire your subordinates, please your peers, and satisfy your boss. Unless your attitudes and behavior impress senior male executives favorably, however, you won't go anywhere.

With that solemn admonition out of the way, I invite you to read on. Like its title, this book has three sections. The suggestions in each section are designed to help you gain access to the executive suite, occupy it with style, and have more fun while you are busy getting there.

Beginning on page 11 you will find brief italicized narratives sprinkled throughout the book. These vignettes are based on actual events, although any resemblance to real individuals or situations is unintended. Mary Louise Hatten, assistant professor of economics at Boston College, and I developed these vignettes to illustrate some of the problems faced by women in business. We use them in seminars, and it has been our experience that men have less trouble finding a solution to the problems than women do. I have included them, not to make you angry, but to make you *think*. *What would you have done?*

THINK LIKE A MAN

To think like a man does not mean that men think better. It means that men think differently. They have been brought up that way. You will improve your chances of succeeding in business, an activity in which male thinking predominates, if you incorporate some of these differences into your own thinking. You may have done so already. If you have, you will know that these ideas compromise neither your intellect nor your femininity. Now, in alphabetical order . . .

ARISTOTLE

This great philosopher said, in a somewhat different context, "Man is the measure of all things." Some give the credit for this insight to Protagoras. Nevertheless, if either of them were to visit a large corporation today, he would see that men make the rules, keep the score, and, for the most part, play the game. It's a fun game. But they won't let you play unless you're very, very good. It's not fair, but you can't change it (within the foreseeable future). Since you have chosen to play in their ball park, have fun, too: learn the rules, learn to keep score, and learn to play the game very, very well.

ASPIRATIONS

One person who never gets bumped from the corporate jet: the Chief Executive Officer (CEO). It's the job with the most fun, most money, and most power to influence other people's lives. It's the only job worth aiming for. It's better to shoot for the CEO job and settle for a senior-management job than to shoot for some middle-management job and find yourself in a dead end. Remember, only the lead dog gets a change of scenery.

BIG PICTURE

What the CEO gets paid for understanding. It is a perspective you should begin to develop. It will distinguish you from your peers who understand only their own jobs. You will understand not only your job, but how it fits in with everybody else's job. As a consequence, you will make better decisions and prepare yourself for the CEO job.

CAREER

Not to be confused with a job (set of activities for which you get paid), a career is a planned, timed sequence of work and work-related experiences that leads you into and through a series of positions in preparation for the ultimate position to which you aspire. Do your job. Focus on your career.

CLUBS

Look for clubs (and associations) that female managers join. Join them. Look for clubs that male managers join. Join them, too. Your club can be a great place to entertain business associates, especially when it's important that you pick up the tab.

COMPANY POLICIES

You are paid to administer them, not complain about them. Criticizing company policies in front of your subordinates is equivalent to knocking top management. Doing that is an invitation to your subordinates to knock you. Instead, learn how company policies influence the behavior of your subordinates and manage accordingly.

COMPANY STOCK

Unless you are trying to take over the company, or your next promotion puts you on the board, don't tie up more than 10 per cent of your net worth in the company's stock. When the stock price goes down (as it will do from time to time), your enthusiasm for your job may go down with it.

COMPETITION

It's the motivation behind all games (especially business) that men play. They get a lot of experience at winning and losing. They learn how to do both with style and grace (or they don't get to play). You must learn to win without bragging and lose without complaining (or you won't get to play).

CONFIDENCES

Once you get a reputation for keeping secrets you will become a warehouse of useful (to you) information. Never violate a confidence. If you do, it will eventually become known that you have. No one will ever tell you anything of value again. Nor will anyone trust or respect you.

CREDIT (Getting)

Don't let others take credit for your ideas or your work. But if you have to choose between getting credit for what's yours and getting the results you want, opt for the latter every time.

CREDIT (Giving)

Make sure your subordinates get credit for what they do. It's not altruism. It's smart business. It builds loyalty.

CRITICISM

Good managers praise in public, criticize in private. Remember, it is your behavior that is being criticized, not you. Once you can accept that fact, criticism becomes a learning experience. Welcome all learning experiences.

DESKS

Make sure yours is at least as big and as expensive as your peers'. Then look at the desk of the most senior male executive in your office. Chances are, there is practically nothing on it except the usual desk blotter, penholder, calendar-clock, and so on. Keep the top of your desk just as neat as his.

DORIS

The discussion about the purchasing contract was going poorly. The raw-material supplier, an elderly president of a family-held company, directed all his comments and questions to Jim. When Doris attempted to point out that she was in charge of the negotiation and that Jim was present only to ensure that the contract was legally proper, the potential supplier became visibly annoyed. She heard him mutter, "You'd think they'd send a real businessman who knew what this thing was all about."

EFFICIENCY

Effectiveness is doing the right thing. Efficiency is doing the thing right. Make sure of the former before concentrating on the latter. It's dumb to spend your time trying to do the wrong thing well. It's even dumber to spend your time trying to do things that don't need to be done at all. Remember the handyman's credo: "If it ain't broke, don't fix it."

EFFORT

You don't get paid for effort. You get paid for results.

EXECUTIVE SUITE

Getting there is half the fun. And if you can negotiate the quicksand, forest fires, and hostile natives, the real and psychic rewards of the executive suite are the same for women as they are for men. Maybe even a little bit better. You weren't expected to make it.

EXPERIENCE

Wise people respect it. Fools rely on it. It always comes in second behind a better idea.

FUN

If you are not enjoying yourself in the job, and you see no prospect for enjoying yourself in it in the near future, get another job. If a job isn't fun, you can't perform it well. So it isn't doing you or your career any good to stay in it. Life is too short to do anything you don't like doing for too long.

GETTING AHEAD

Successful people get ahead because of their intellect, energy, determination, character, interpersonal skill, charisma, and luck. None of these characteristics is a sex-linked phenomenon.

GOLDEN HANDCUFFS

What the company retirement plan can become if you let it. Unless you're over sixty, you can *always* afford to leave a job. Don't trade your career for an annuity.

HEALTHY ORGANIZATIONS

In healthy organizations, the successful people (those who receive the tangible and intangible rewards) are competent (perform their jobs well), and the competent people are successful. In unhealthy organizations, the successful people are incompetent, and the competent people are unsuccessful. It is hard enough for a competent woman to get ahead in a healthy organization, let alone an unhealthy one. If you work for the latter, get out!

HELP

With the possible exception of talking when you should be listening, nothing will cause you more trouble than the tranquil consciousness of your effortless superiority. When you need help, recognize it and ask for it.

HERACLITUS

This great philosopher observed that you can't step in the same stream twice. Since you can't take back the past, don't fret over mistakes. Good executives take responsibility for them, learn from them, and go on with their work.

HEROES

Most men have heroes. They talk about them all the time. These heroes tend to be local or national sports figures. Learn who they are. If you live in Cincinnati or Philadelphia and think Pete Rose is a flower, you've got a serious problem.

HIRING

Try to hire people better than you. Highly competent employees will make your job easier and your promotion more certain. If one of them leapfrogs over you, you will have gained a competent boss and, perhaps, another good friend.

HONESTY

If you want to get to the top, honesty is not the *best* policy. It's the *only* policy.

JEALOUSY

Think of it as a perverted form of respect. It's the emotion that the incompetent people reserve for the competent ones.

JOAN

By 9:10 A.M. on the first day at her new assignment as district sales manager—the first woman to be promoted to that position in the company—Joan felt the new pressures of her job. Her office was around the corner from the offices of the three other district sales managers. Furthermore, the office was obviously carved out of unused open space and was still being constructed. One wall was fiberboard, with the carpenter's figures still readable in black grease paint. Arlene, the secretary she shared with the three other managers, said in baby talk, "Don't worry, sweetie, your office will be painted right away. Do you want pink?"

JOB HOPPING

Normally, it's bad practice to stay with a company for fewer than two years. Your résumé will look like an airline schedule. When another company really wants you, however, consider the offer carefully. Don't leave a good job for anything less than a 30 per cent salary increase or a *fantastic* opportunity.

JOB SELECTION

Top executives develop a kind of humble self-confidence from mastering a variety of situations and surviving a variety of mistakes. The only way you can get that kind of self-confidence is by being in a job where your performance is measured against quantitative criteria. You don't need to prove yourself to others as much as you need to prove yourself to yourself. Get a *line* job.

LANGUAGE (Male)

Men have a special shorthand language system they use with one another. You must learn to understand it. For instance, if a male co-worker says to you, "I'm going to lunch," that is an invitation. Your correct response should be, "I'll be right with you." If you had waited for him to add, "Do you want to come along?" you'd end up eating lunch all by yourself. If he says, "How's it going?" when both you and he know you're about to fall behind on a project deadline, that's an offer. Your correct response should be, "I could use a little help." If you had waited for him to add, "You looked swamped. Can I help bail you out?" you'd have missed the deadline all by yourself.

LEADERSHIP

It's best to think of it as an activity, not an attribute. That way, you'll start doing it instead of wondering whether you can. People will start following you when they (1) know where you're going; (2) want to go with you; and (3) know you will help them get there. Leaders are vital to the success of any enterprise. The speed of the leader is the speed of the pack.

LINE JOBS

The only kind to have. If you are not making it or selling it, or managing those who do, you are an overhead item, an expense, a drain on profits. The action, the fun, the excitement, the glory, the money are all in the line jobs. So is the power.

LINE PERSONNEL

These are the players in the game. They make decisions. Staff personnel make recommendations. You usually get paid a lot more for making decisions than for making recommendations.

LOYALTY (To your boss)

This virtue is highly prized by men. It is not only expected of you, it is required. It is easy to be loyal to a competent boss. It is hard to be loyal to an incompetent one. Nevertheless, you *must*. Remember, "If you can't say nothin' nice, don't say nothin' at all!"

LOYALTY (To your company)

Don't carry it too far. Remember, you are exchanging your labor (your job) for money (your salary). Don't confuse your job with your career. You owe the company a day's work for a day's pay. You don't have to let it control your life. If another company offers you a job more in line with your career aspirations, and the salary seems a fair exchange for your labor, take it.

LOYALTY (To your subordinates)

Their loyalty to you will never be greater than your loyalty to them.

MANAGERIAL BEHAVIOR

Your value system should always control your behavior. Your behavior should be a function of the situation and what it calls for, the people involved in the situation, and the relationships between and among them. A good manager has the ability to make appropriate behavior modifications without compromising his or her value system.

MEN

By and large, men are a decent lot. A small percentage are sympathetic, knowledgeable, and anxious for women to succeed. These men make good bosses and, when in positions of influence, make good mentors. A much larger percentage are sympathetic, but not particularly knowledgeable. These men can be educated and their sense of fair play can be relied upon to give you a chance to succeed. An unfortunately large percentage are basically hostile to your presence, but won't do much more than try to "keep you in your place." These men will probably never change, so just take care to treat them politely and professionally. A small percentage are *sick*. Learn to avoid this last group.

MENTORS

Nearly all men who achieve positions of influence have been helped by senior men who spotted their talent; coached, counseled, encouraged, and protected them; and used their own influence to advance their protégés' careers. Women need mentors, too. A few men will take on this role for a woman. And so will some senior women executives. These men and women are the *true* professionals who are interested in developing *people*. If you have a mentor, maintain the relationship. You *cannot* choose one. The mentor will be attracted to you by your competence, character, energy, and ambition.

MYTHOLOGY

Business is riddled with uncritically held beliefs. Avoid them. Some of the most prevalent mythologies are: "We've always done it this way." "It won't work." "Men will . . ." "Women can't . . ."

NETWORKS

Men spend a lot of time and energy cultivating and keeping friends and acquaintances. Men readily ask for favors and grant them to one another based on these contacts. Thus, deals are made, jobs are found, and information is shared among these "old boy" networks. You should be building your own network. Stay in contact with every fellow alumna, female co-worker, and woman manager you meet. Don't exclude men, either. Follow the male example: feel free to ask for favors; feel free to grant them.

OFFICE

Make sure yours is as big and as well equipped as your peers'. Your office is more than your work space, it is your position in the organization. It should be located where the action is, not around the corner. It should be kept as neat and efficient-looking as your boss's. Don't make it look "feminine" or "homey." Avoid African violets.

OUTSIDE INTERESTS

Don't marry your job. Outside interests enrich your social life, your intellectual life, and your spiritual life. All these enrichments make you a better manager. They give you perspective.

PAULA

Paula had worked hard preparing for her first annual salary and performance review. She entered her boss's office and sat down. The file folder on her lap contained documentation that she had saved the division over $80,000 in her negotiations with OSHA officials. She believed that this achievement, together with the letter of congratulations from the division manager, should be worth a $4,000 raise over her current $18,000 annual salary. In addition, she had learned from a friend in the accounting department that one of her co-workers had had his salary raised from $20,000 to $22,000. This individual had joined the company at the same time as Paula but was generally considered a "goof-off." Her boss began by saying, "I must apologize for not putting in as much time on your review as I did on the men in the department. I know their interest in the appraisal is greater than yours would be. For one thing, they're all married. You have done a good job. I think a $2,000 raise is justified in your case and that's what I'm putting in for you."

PEOPLE

If you don't like and respect people in general and co-workers in particular, you will never become a good manager. You can't manage people you don't like and respect. If you have a hang-up about liking and respecting men, get rid of it. If you can't manage men, you'll never succeed. Period.

PERKS

In the military, the visible signs of rank are sewn on the uniforms. In business, they take the form of perquisites. Some are subtle, such as the quality of the draperies in your office; others are not, such as country club memberships. Get *all* the perks your position offers. Don't let yourself be outranked if you want to be taken seriously.

POLITICS (Office)

Not for you. These games are played by incompetents who cannot compete except by trying to undercut the competents. But learn who these players are. Avoid them if you can. In healthy organizations, they seldom succeed for very long.

POPULAR

It's nice to be. And it's possible to be outstanding and popular, too. But aim first for the former. Remember, popularity is the *only* reward for mediocrity.

POWER

There is no reason women can't wield it. But it takes time, skill, and effort to get it. Having it means that people will do what you want them to do. Power comes from four sources— *charisma:* people want to be associated with you and what you stand for; *position:* people acknowledge your right to command; *resources:* people want what you have to give; and *information:* people want to know what you know. Developing one source isn't enough. You must develop all four sources. Remember, however, the responsibility that goes with power is awesome.

PRAISE

Don't expect it. Never ask for it. If you are doing a good job, you will hear nothing. If you are doing a poor job, you will hear something quite soon. If you know you are doing a poor job and you hear nothing, update your résumé.

PROMOTIONS

Keep your boss fully aware of your desire to be promoted. Discuss with him or her the career path options available and what you have to do to qualify—then get qualified. Keep your eyes and ears open. When you hear of an opening that fits into your career strategy, throw your hat into the ring—ask to be considered. Supply proof of your qualifications. If you are turned down, ask for the reasons. If they don't sound logical (or legal), raise hell. A man would, and you'll be admired for it. The next time around, you will be considered seriously.

PROTÉGÉS

Once you get there, turn around and look behind you. You'll see lots of bright young people who need a mentor.

RAISES

If you are not getting them fast enough, ask for them. The company is not going to give you anything you don't ask for. Several weeks before your department's budget is to be settled, document the reasons why you deserve a raise, determine how much you think it should be, and inform your boss—calmly and graciously—what you expect it to be. You have nothing to lose. If the boss agrees, you win. If the boss doesn't agree, you (1) gain the opportunity to present your case; (2) may get a compromise; (3) call attention to your interest in getting ahead; and (4) evidence that you are "thinking like a man."

RESILIENCE

Bounce back from your losses, disappointments, and frustrations. Many men gain resilience from experience in team sports. They learn to accept that "You can't win 'em all." Accept that fact, too. And learn the follow-up: "We'll get 'em next time."

RESPONSIBILITY

It's what you are after. It's fun to have it. Grab every bit of it you can. Remember, though: a manager can delegate authority; a manager can never delegate responsibility. So, once you have grabbed it, be prepared to see it through.

RISK

All business decisions involve risk. There's a downside and an upside. If you are preoccupied with the downside, your career will never be much fun. If you focus on the upside, your career will be a lot of fun and you will make better decisions. Keep your eye on the doughnut, not on the hole.

ROME

It wasn't built in a day. Neither will your career be. So, be patient. But don't be passive. Learn the difference.

SALARIES (Yours)

The salary you earn means more to you than just the money you receive. It signals your position in the hierarchy of employees. If your value to the company is greater than your position in this hierarchy, you will be taken for a sucker. Make sure you are being paid *at least as much* as others (read: MEN) in your position.

SALLY

Sally was angry and disappointed as she heard her boss tell her that she was not to be included in the group that was going to the trade association meeting in New Orleans next month. He continued, "We all recognize that you have done most of the 'inside work' on the presentation, but we really don't need you at the meeting. Besides, having you along will create a problem. Jim's wife is upset about his being out of town with you. And Fred and Bill think you will put a damper on their evening activities. You can see their point of view, can't you?"

SECURITY

Not something to shoot for. You already carry around the only kind of security you can ever have. It's the gray stuff that occupies the space between your ears.

SELLING

It's great experience. No one will know the realities of the company's products, customers, or competitors any better than you will. In addition to this valuable knowledge, you will gain in persistence, patience, persuasiveness, and self-confidence. All these qualities make you a better manager.

SOMERSET MAUGHAM

You'll win some. You'll lose some. You'll have good days. You'll have bad days. Don't let it get you down. Keep your enthusiasm up. Remember what Somerset Maugham said: "Only mediocre people are always at their best."

SPORT TALK

Learn to understand it. Otherwise you will get boxed out, blitzed, hit below the belt, and find yourself out in left field.

STAFF JOBS

Only good for six-month stints. Valuable for rest and recuperation from the excitement of line jobs and, sometimes, to learn a new skill. They are to be avoided like the plague under all other circumstances. Staff people are the equivalent of cheerleaders, trainers, scorekeepers, spectators, and referees. The real game is played on the field by those holding the line jobs. That is where you want to be.

STAMINA

If men have any advantage over women, it's in their physical strength. This attribute shows up as stamina: the ability to go flat out for hours at a time. You must be able to keep up with them. Stay in shape. Eat properly. Exercise regularly. And get the right amount of sleep.

TEAM WORK

Most activities in organizations are carried out by groups of people working together. Your accomplishments as an individual are seldom as important to your career success as your contribution to the various teams for which you play. Business activity is a football game, not a figure-skating contest. Forget that fact and you will be doing your figure eights in the Food Stamp line.

TRUST

You can't go through life sleeping with one eye open. You can't go through life being ripped off, either. Learning whom to trust is one of life's great adventures. You'll make mistakes. Everybody does. But don't make the same mistake twice. If someone betrays your trust, don't give him or her a chance to do it again.

VALUES

The easy decisions in business can be solved by analysis. The difficult ones require value judgments. Try to hire people whose values are similar to yours. That way, your subordinates' decisions will be similar to yours. Your subordinates will also be easier to trust.

WORD (Yours)

Millions of dollars are exchanged every day on the strength of the spoken word. A gentleman's word is his bond. So must yours be. If you have given your word on a deal, and a better one comes along, you can't renege. If you do, your word will be worthless. You will have forfeited your integrity.

WORRY

Successful executives confine this activity to situations over which they have some control. Worrying about things over which you have no control is a sign of immaturity.

ACT LIKE A LADY

To act like a lady does not mean that you should look and behave stereotypically. It means that you should look and behave professionally. For you to succeed in business, your associates must be comfortable in your presence and receptive to your competence. The suggestions below will help you achieve these goals.

AMUSEMENT

The emotion you should feel when someone mistakes you for a secretary. Anger is a luxury. It should be reserved for only the most severe instances of injustice.

ANTICIPATION

Learn to anticipate potentially ugly situations. Working late, office mistletoe, and conventions are particularly dangerous. When you spot the first drunk, leave the party. It won't get any better.

ASSERTIVENESS

Life doesn't give you anything you don't ask for. People won't pay attention to things you don't say. Some women have trouble learning how to assert themselves effectively. Society typically doesn't give women as much chance to practice as it gives men. Here are a few things that generally work: stick to logical arguments; keep voice and manner calm; don't back off; acknowledge opposing views with grace and understanding.

BANGLES

Along with baubles and bright, shiny beads, bangles should not be worn to work. They're distracting. A good watch, a good ring, unobtrusive earrings, and a thin gold necklace are usually sufficient. A single pin, if it is *very good*, is okay, too.

BEAUTIFUL

If you are, send your parents a thank-you note and then get back to work.

BETH

Beth picked up her briefcase and started to walk over toward her colleagues. Today she had been involved in a formal presentation to a prospective customer, along with her boss, the district sales manager, and representatives from engineering, manufacturing, and distribution. Beth thought the presentation was outstanding. It had taken all day, and although her part in it was small, she was happy with the way she had handled herself. As she walked over to join the group that had clustered in the corridor outside the conference room, the customer's marketing vice-president, next to whom she had sat at lunch, came over to her and said, "How about dinner tonight? Oh, don't worry. I checked with your boss, and it's okay with him."

BOOTS

Good for horseback riding and getting to and from work during inclement weather. Not good for the office unless you want to look like a Prussian field marshal. Or you get a kick out of men wondering where you keep your whip.

BRILLIANT

Even if you are, try not to show it too often. Brilliant people make the rest of us nervous. We call them "erratic." The words you want people to use to describe you are "competent," "energetic," "dependable," "professional," and "good team player."

CHECK (Paying)

To avoid situations that are likely to produce a tug of war over the check, make your restaurant preparations in advance. (It helps to choose a restaurant in which you're known.) Make the reservation in your name and specify you want the check. Tell the headwaiter when you get there. Give the waiter your credit card as he takes orders for coffee.

CHECK (Splitting)

Make every effort to pay your own way, especially with male co-workers. Most of these situations will be cash deals, with everyone scrounging to come up with the right change. Be prepared. Always carry lots of singles. You will be the only one able to make the right change.

CIRCUIT BREAKERS

A little sexual electricity crackling in the air is normal between men and women. It's no different in business. But be on your guard against power surges. Master the use of circuit breakers: ways to say "no" without making a man feel defective or degenerate. If you don't know at least a dozen ways, learn them.

CLIENTS/CUSTOMERS

All the rules that apply to male co-workers apply equally to *all* males you meet while working. Your reputation in your field is even more important than your reputation in your company. Your career in the former can never be shorter than your career in the latter.

CLOTHING

The importance of dressing well, and appropriately, cannot be overemphasized. Remember, your male boss probably spends $300 on each of his suits. And he probably has a dozen of them. Don't be afraid to go first class when it comes to your wardrobe. *What* to wear is a more difficult decision. Women currently have no arbiter such as a Brooks Brothers. You are probably on target if men with whom you work say, "That's a *great*-looking outfit you're wearing," but probably off target if they say, "You look *great* in that outfit."

COMPANY PICNICS

If you must attend, you want to avoid looking like a temptress (to wives) or a temptation (to lonely males). So always be accompanied by a (non–fellow employee) man. If you are single, the ideal date has a body like Mr. Universe's and a face like Lee Marvin's.

CONNIE

It was the Monday of Connie's second week on the job. She had spent the weekend fixing up her new apartment, and the idea of being completely on her own for the first time was just beginning to dawn on her. She looked up from the pile of papers on her desk and saw Jim, another of the twelve salesmen in her district, walking over to her. Jim said, "Isn't it about time you began to get around and see what our fair city has to offer in the way of night life? How about having dinner with me on Friday night, and maybe taking in a show?"

COPING

Common sense dictates that it is wise to anticipate and avoid ugly situations. On the other hand, you can't live your life in a cocoon. If you can't approach new and ambiguous situations with zest and élan, your managerial life will be one of quiet desperation. Exploring and mastering new situations is fun. It also does wonders for your self-esteem.

COURTESY (Female)

Why do women put each other down when men are so much better at it? Treat your female co-workers with respect. Don't be quick to find fault with them. Men stick together. Women should, too. If you must talk about other women, talk about their strong points. The same goes for talking about men.

COURTESY (Male)

No man is putting you down by holding a door open for you or by standing up when you join his table. Accept graciously all such courtesies (exception: see LUGGAGE). Senior male executives, in particular, will confer them upon you automatically and be very upset if you are not gracious about accepting them.

CRYING

Like applying lipstick, crying should be done in private. Control yourself. Very few men can accept crying for what it is: a legitimate form for expressing emotions. Most businessmen view a woman's crying as either an attempt to manipulate them or evidence of "feminine inferiority." Either way, you lose.

CULTURE

Take advantage of every drop of culture your community offers. If all you can talk about is yourself and your job, you will bore everyone around you to death. The further you progress up the ladder, the more multidimensional you need to become. A knowledge and appreciation of good books, good music, and good art add important dimensions to you and to your career.

DATING

Don't date fellow employees. If you date one and it becomes known, the rumors will have you sleeping with him. Fair game for one is fair game for all, meaning that you will have every self-styled stud in the place hanging around your office. Worse yet, senior management will hear the rumors and your chances for promotion will be zero! The same rule holds for men, but the risk in disregarding this advice is much lower. If a great relationship does come along disguised as a fellow employee, one of you should resume your career elsewhere.

DINNER (Alone)

Check out the dining room. If it looks crummy, bring something to read so you won't be establishing eye contact with traveling salesmen. Better yet, try room service. If the dining room looks nice, forget the reading material and enjoy your meal. If you can't cope with an unwanted approach with grace and style, learn how to.

DINNER (Business)

Don't let it turn into a date. Stick to one drink. Avoid dessert. Whether having dinner with a single business associate or a group, be the first to leave. If you hang around, it looks as if you are expecting to be entertained or, even worse, to be the entertainment. Exception: if it is a business dinner and you are one of several businesswomen in the group, be the *last* businesswoman to leave. Chances are, after you leave, no further business will be discussed.

DRINKING

Civilization is a thin veneer. It rapidly dissolves in alcohol. *Never, ever,* have more than one drink in public. More careers have been ruined by booze than by incompetence.

ELEGANCE

The way you pay a compliment, return a favor, ask for a day off, or handle an unwanted advance can't be learned from a book. Elegance is a personal quality unique to you. It can be developed only through observation, experimentation, and determination. It's one quality where practice not only makes perfect, it makes friends.

ENTERTAINING

Check around before throwing a party involving co-workers. Let the company's social norms suggest the answers to the following: Do I invite the boss or other superiors? What about subordinates? Are guests expected to reciprocate? In general, it's best to err on the side of too little entertaining than too much. Being a professional doesn't require being a Perle Mesta.

ETHEL

As Ethel Wilson, product manager for Acme Foods, prepared to leave the stall in the ladies' room, she overheard two secretaries talking about her.

The first one said, "That Ethel Wilson sure spends a lot of time in Mr. Evans' office. And she doesn't even work for him!"

The other replied, "I know. It's all over the building. I can't blame her, though. I wouldn't mind having an affair with a vice-president."

Ethel didn't know whether to open the door and come out or stand there until they left. And if she did decide to come out, what was she going to say?

ETHICS

If the deal doesn't smell good, it won't taste good.

FACE (Yours)

Distinguish between facial actions and expressions that are automatic and those that are natural. Work hard to get rid of the former. Most people are uncomfortable in the presence of someone who nods in response to every statement, walks around smiling all the time, or laughs at every joke. You want to be a manager, not a mannequin. Use a nod to indicate agreement. Use a smile to express pleasure. Use a laugh to compliment humor.

FAVORS

Always acknowledge a favor. If you appear pleased and surprised by favors, everybody feels good. If you appear to expect them, you are inviting unequal treatment elsewhere.

FEMININITY

Find your personal line between being feminine and being seductive, and don't cross it. You should be and have every right in business to be the former; you should not be and have no right in business to be the latter.

GENTLEMEN

You can't always tell them by their manners. But they are easy to spot. Gentlemen never willingly or unnecessarily inflict pain. Women who exhibit this same behavior are called ladies.

GIFT (Expensive)

If a male co-worker or business associate gives you one, either marry him or return it.

GOSSIP

Listen to it; don't spread it.

GOSSIP (About you)

Ignore it. If unfounded, it will eventually dry up and blow away. If you actively attempt to dispel it, you will only keep it alive longer. If a friend tells you about it, say "That's ridiculous." Then change the subject. Don't ask a friend to dispel it, either. A good friend will.

HAIR

Stick to hair styles that look neat and tidy. Remember, your male boss gets *his* hair cut every two weeks.

HANDS (Male)

They should not linger *anywhere* on your body. Get them off quickly! The hand on your waist is just six inches away from an ugly scene. Say something that will discourage him without rejecting him. Or move away abruptly. He should get the idea.

HANDS (Yours)

Don't use them to fuss with your hair or pick at your clothes while talking or listening to people. It makes you look nervous. Keep your unoccupied hands below your waist while standing and in your lap or on your chair arms while sitting. And for goodness' sake, keep them off co-workers!

HELEN KELLER

Someone to think about the next time you feel sorry for yourself or are about to say, "It's not fair."

HEMLINE

Pay careful attention to the length of your skirts. In most fashion years, if your hemlines are too short, you'll be mistaken for your boss's secretary; if they're too long, you'll be mistaken for your boss's mother.

HIGH FASHION

Unless you're in the fashion business, high fashion is not the way to dress for work. It looks as if you just stopped in on your way to a party. Or didn't bother to go home after the one last night.

HONEY

Unless it happens to be your name, don't let your co-workers use this term when addressing you. If used to put you down, be firm: "My name is Jane." If used casually, take a lighter approach: "Are you talking to me?"

HUMOR

An antidote for stress. A lubricant for relations between and among people. No wonder a sense of humor is so highly prized in the business world. If you've got it, flaunt it!

JARGON

Words like "finalize" and "interface" have no place in your vocabulary. Jargon makes you sound as if you are "playing at" business.

LANGUAGE (Anglo-Saxon)

Words like "bullshit" are the *exclusive* property of men. You can be a competent member of the team. You can never be "one of the boys." Don't even try. You have nothing to gain by using coarse language and, if overheard by a senior male executive, everything to lose.

LIES

Never lie to protect yourself. The *only* excuse for lying is to protect someone else. Even then, don't tell more than one such lie a year. No one has a good enough memory to be a successful liar.

LUGGAGE

If a male co-worker with whom you are traveling offers to carry your suitcase, decline cheerfully and graciously. Carry your own luggage or pay a porter to do it. Travel light. Never put more in a suitcase than you can carry at a quick pace for a hundred yards. Nothing will make you look quite as incompetent to your male co-workers as lugging something that is obviously too heavy for you.

MAKE-UP

Don't show up for work looking like the pharaoh's wife. Except for well-groomed eyebrows and lashes, and a carefully applied, understated lipstick, the best make-up is none at all. If you need a little more help, the next best make-up is the kind that looks like none at all.

NAILS

Despite what you read in fashion magazines, long red fingernails are a poor way to express your femininity. Keep your nails as short as possible, consistent with your social life. Keep them even. Use clear or very pale polish.

NAME DROPPING

Ipecac induces nausea and vomiting. Name dropping merely induces nausea.

NAMES (First)

When in doubt, don't use first names unless requested to do so. Use last names to address all people who look more than twenty-five years older than you, regardless of their position or status. If they insist on a first-name relationship, give in and find some other way to confer respect.

NANCY

A group of executives from various companies was attending a seminar conducted by a major university. After cocktails, the newly acquainted fellow participants began dinner. There were sixteen men and one woman in the group. The woman, Nancy Bradley, a loan officer with a prominent bank, sat with Jim Gunter on her left and Bill Thomas on her right.

Midway through dinner, two late arrivals from Chicago joined the dinner party. As they were waiting to be served, introductions began around the table from left to right. Mr. Gunter finished introducing himself to the newcomers and all eyes moved to Nancy. As she started to introduce herself, she heard Mr. Thomas begin, "I'm Bill Thomas." Nancy gave him a startled look, but quickly joined in the laughter as one man said, "Hey, you skipped someone," quickly followed by, "and the most attractive one in the bunch." Mr. Thomas promptly corrected his error by saying, "Oh, yes, she's our entertainment for tonight!"

NECKLINE

Unless you are working in Japan, your neckline should flatter your neck, not your bosom.

OFFICE PARTIES

No one ever "got ahead" as a consequence of attending an office party. Thousands, however, have ruined their chances. A real no-win situation because many companies view attendance at these rituals as obligatory. The only solution is to arrive early and leave at the first sign that the ritual is becoming an orgy.

PEERS

Be friendly and treat them with respect. Outperform them if you can, but never by so much that it makes them look bad. Remember, a peer is both a potential subordinate and a potential boss.

PERFUME

Go easy. The fragrance should complement your presence, not announce it. Avoid perfumes that strongly suggest forests, gardens, citrus fruits, or the exotic glands of furry animals.

PHYSICAL ATTRIBUTES

Make sure that neither your clothes nor your body movements repeatedly call attention to your bosom, your fanny, or your legs. It's better to have a man spend a few seconds speculating about your body than to have him spend all day fantasizing about it. In business you want men listening to you, not looking at you.

POLITICS (Personal)

Like religion, your politics are your own business. The opinions you are paid to express are your professional ones. If your thing is the Women's Movement, do it on your time, not on the company's time.

PRIVATE LIFE

Although your private life is your own business, you don't need to become paranoid about keeping everything about yourself a secret. Share with your co-workers the kind of thing you would share with casual friends (but not necessarily what your co-workers might share with you). You can be professional without being mysterious.

PUNCTUALITY

Keeping men waiting may be part of the mating game. It does not belong in business. Being late for appointments and meetings is rude, inconsiderate, and unprofessional. Don't let them say, "Just like a woman." Be on time.

PUTDOWNS

Eleanor Roosevelt said it best: "No one can make you feel inferior without your consent."

QUID PRO QUO

Don't keep score on people by computing favors given/favors received ratios. You will never be hurt by helping someone or caring for someone as long as you don't expect anything in return.

RAINWEAR

On those days that you really need to look your professional best, it will usually rain. Make sure you stay dry. Spend as much on your raincoat (and matching rain hat) as you would on your winter coat. Keep a good folding umbrella in your briefcase.

SHAKING HANDS

A must among men at all appropriate occasions. So you must, too. Try to be the first to offer a hand. A courteous male is torn between offering you his first because the business situation calls for it, and not offering it first because it may be considered bad manners. By going first, you remove the awkwardness. Remember, you want men to feel comfortable in your presence, not tense.

SHOES

If a man stares at your feet, don't conclude that he's a fetishist. More likely, your shoes are either inappropriate or scruffy. *His* are shined.

SIMONE DE BEAUVOIR

When someone criticizes you for being "aggressive," remember the words of this extraordinary woman: "There are two kinds of people: human beings and women. And when women start acting like human beings, they are accused of trying to be men."

SMOKING

If you must light up in someone else's office, ask permission first. Never enter someone else's office carrying a cigarette. Better still, quit smoking altogether.

STUPIDITY

Don't confuse it with ignorance. Stupid people deserve your compassion. They were born that way. Ignorant people deserve your attention. They can be educated.

SUITS

Worn with blouses, suits are the professional thing to wear to work. Unless your organization has a lot of successful women managers who wear pantsuits, stick to skirted suits. You want to look feminine, not "functional." Wear pantsuits only for traveling.

SWEATERS

Wear them while skiing, not while working.

TAILORING

No matter how much you spent on that jacket, if it doesn't fit properly, particularly through the shoulders, everyone will notice. Good clothes mean fit and fabric, in that order. Take your good jacket to a good tailor and spend a few bucks to make it look good.

THANK YOU

The most beautiful expression in the English language. Use it whenever you can.

TIPPING

Women get a bum rap as tippers. Blame it on the little old ladies who frequent tearooms. Give porters fifty cents a bag. Give taxi drivers, bartenders, and waiters 15 per cent if the service is okay and 20 per cent if it's really good. Don't concern yourself about the small army that waits on you in fancy restaurants. It divvies up your tip.

TOUGHNESS

Discover for yourself your own personal line between being tough and being hard, and don't cross it. Toughness, the ability to dish it out and take it without complaining, is expected of you. Hardness, the ability to be tough without feeling or caring, is not only unfeminine, it is inhuman.

VOCABULARY

Avoid big words when small ones will do. There are better ways to demonstrate your competence than by substituting "vagary" for "whim." If you must use a big word, make sure you're pronouncing it correctly.

VOICE

Don't raise yours unless the building's on fire.

WARMTH (Personal)

The management of personal warmth is perhaps the most difficult aspect of being a woman in business. It is potentially your biggest plus and your biggest minus. Too little warmth and you won't be liked. Too much warmth and you won't be taken seriously.

WEIGHT

Remember how old you were when you were really proud of how you looked? How much did you weigh? Get to and stay within five pounds of that weight. Every pound in excess of that number is shortening your life and reducing your effectiveness as a manager. Did you ever see a *fat* CEO?

WIVES

Try to meet the wives of the men you work with. Some will like you (they also have careers); some will admire you (they wish they had careers); some will envy you (they also wish they had careers but are less self-confident); some will pity you (for "having to work"); and some will feel threatened by you (that's their problem, about which you can do nothing, so forget it). The best way to meet them is in their own homes, so don't turn down this kind of invitation. The next best way is in your home, if you are married. (It can be awkward if you are not.) The third best way is to throw a party and invite several co-workers and their wives. The worst way is at company social functions. But it's better than not meeting them at all.

ZOO

What your office will become if you blow kisses at or hug male co-workers.

WORK LIKE A DOG

To work like a dog does not mean that you should exhaust yourself in unproductive activities. It means that you should work smart. Who gets more (food, shelter, and attention) for doing less (wagging its tail) than a dog?

AIRPORTS

Missed flights and bad connections can force you to spend time alone in the worst possible place except a bus terminal: an airport. Keep track of the airports you visit the most, the airlines you fly the most, and get yourself one or more airline lounge memberships (e.g., American's Admirals Club). Airline lounges are good places to work or rest in relative privacy.

ANSWERING SERVICE

A good idea if you can afford it. Give the number to your friends and ask them to use it instead of calling you at work.

ASSISTANT TO

The worst job in the company. If you are any good, your boss won't let you go; if you are not, no one else in the organization will have you. You can't become a manager by flashing someone else's badge.

BLAME

When something goes wrong most people will be looking for someone to blame. You should be looking for some way to fix it.

BOSSES

Treat with respect. Bosses are the most important people in your working life. Assume bosses may know something you don't. Never get angry with them; they may be testing you. Make them proud of you and they will talk you up to their bosses. That's how you get promoted.

BOSSES (Female)

Few bosses are. Don't put her on a pedestal just because she's a woman. Chances are, she's likely to be more competent than her male counterparts. But don't count on it. It is worse to work for a bad female boss than a bad male boss. You both get blamed for her mistakes.

BOSSES (Good ones)

Try to work for one who is never satisfied with less than your best, always available to teach you a better way to do it, and completely candid with you. A good boss is interested in you, your career, and your performance, in reverse order. If you don't have a good boss, move heaven and earth to get one.

BOSSES (Male)

Most bosses are. Remember, he is not your father, he is not your brother, he is not your husband, he is not your boyfriend. Don't expect him to behave like any of the above. Even more important, don't encourage him to behave like any of the above.

BRIEFCASE

Decide what you want to spend on a briefcase. Then buy one that costs twice as much. Make sure it's leather. Make sure it's functional for what you need to carry.

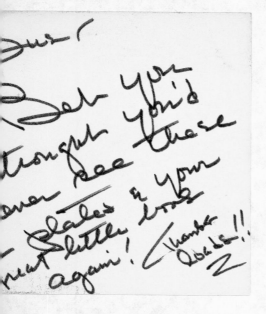

BUSINESS CARDS (Other people's)

Collect them. Write on the back how, where, and when you got them. File them.

BUSINESS CARDS (Yours)

Not for internal use. Instead, make sure people in your company know who you are and what you do by meeting them. Business cards are for external use only. Pass them out. They aren't doing you or your company any good in your wallet.

CALENDAR

Get yourself a desk calendar you can write on. Use it for your daily planning. Use it to post all written and oral deadline agreements and promises, yours and other people's. Use it to post all co-workers' birthdays and company anniversary dates.

CHAOS

A common situation in business. Don't panic. Take it one step at a time. Reduce chaos to confusion. Convert confusion to disorganization. Slow down disorganization to inertia. Capitalize on inertia to create organization. Use organization to build momentum. Ride momentum to encourage initiative. Reward initiative to achieve creativity. Then look around for more chaos.

CHILDREN

His career does not prevent a man from becoming a father. Yours need not prevent you from becoming a mother. If you've thought seriously about both the joys and responsibilities children bring and you want them, go ahead. Like a man, you will need to make chaos-proof child-care arrangements for your time at work. Live-in housekeepers are probably the best answer. Except in extreme emergencies, don't use children as an excuse for non-performance. If you want to be treated as a professional, you have to behave like a professional. Life for women managers with children is more complicated, but it's exciting to overhear your children tell their friends, "My mom's a vice-president."

CHITCHAT

An important source of information and a good way to cement your position on "the team." Nevertheless, it can eat up your day if you let it get out of hand. The answer is to budget time for it and work it into your daily schedule.

CREDIT CARDS

You need three: American Express (for charging business items); Visa or Master Charge (for charging personal items); and one major oil company card. An executive's sophistication is inversely related to the number of credit cards he or she carries.

DEAD END

Any job "traditionally" held by a woman. Also, any job you have held for three years or more.

DEADLINES

Make them and you will earn the most prized appellation in business: "dependable." Miss them and it's back to the salt mines.

DELEGATION

It is better to struggle with a sick jackass than carry the wood yourself. Successful executives hire and train good people, give them something important to do, and motivate them to do it. Don't get bogged down by trying to do everything yourself or by doing things you pay others to do.

DISPLEASURE

From time to time you will find it necessary to indicate your displeasure at another person's performance. Most often, it will be to a subordinate. Criticizing others requires skill. Avoid making it personal. Talk about the *behavior* you find unsatisfactory, not about the attitudes or attributes that produced the behavior. Don't procrastinate. Call unsatisfactory performance to the individual's attention as soon as you can do it in private. Never criticize people without showing them how you want it done or how they can do it better.

EXERCISE

Your body carries your brain around. Take care of it. Get plenty of exercise—at least one hour, three times a week. You'll feel better, look better, and have more energy for your work.

EXPENSE ACCOUNT

If you're on one, let your client/customer know it. Any resistance to your picking up the lunch or dinner check will evaporate.

FACE (Other person's)

Words are but one way we communicate with one another. Our facial expressions are another. Good eye contact, both when listening *and* when talking, allows you to understand better what the speaker is saying and to perceive better what the listener is hearing.

FIRED

An antonym for "hired." Clerks are fired. Professionals "leave to find greater opportunities elsewhere." No matter how defined, when it happens to you, it's a shock. Remember, unless your boss hates you, he or she is probably feeling guilty. Accept termination with grace. Learn the reasons why. Get a specific termination date. Ask about separation pay (the company's conscience money). Ask for a letter of recommendation. Leave the company with style and class. Getting fired is not the end of the world. It's the beginning of a new journey. Never tell interviewers you were fired. It's none of their business.

FRIEDA

*Three young women, students at a leading graduate busi-
ness school, were having lunch together. After a brief discussion about the morning's classes, Frieda, the youngest,
said, "Mind if I ask you two about job interviews? I am having trouble answering some of the recruiters' questions. For
instance, what do you say when they ask you if you have
any plans to get married?"*

*"That question is similar to the one I get asked when they
spot my engagement ring," said Wendy. "What do I say
when they suggest that I come back and talk to them when
I get my personal life settled?"*

*"I get a lot of questions about my husband's plans,"
added Jane. "I don't know what to say either. I feel like saying that it's none of their damn business! It really makes me
mad, though, when they ask me to tell them when I expect
to have children."*

GENERALIZATIONS

Avoid them, particularly in reference to men and women. Generalizations are the sloppiest short cut in thinking. They cause bum decisions. Memorize the following: "All Indians walk in single file; at least, the one I saw did."

GOETHE

This great poet-philosopher observed that "There is nothing more frightful than ignorance in action." Have this saying lettered and framed. Hang it on the wall in your office opposite your desk. Read it several times a day. Think of it before you shoot from the hip.

HANDBAG

Avoid carrying both a handbag *and* a briefcase. Instead, buy small flat handbags that fit inside your briefcase. That way, when you don't need your briefcase—at lunch, for instance—you carry only your handbag. When you do need your briefcase, your handbag is inside, easily accessible.

HANDWRITING

Unless you want people to think you're a doctor, take pains to write legibly. Forcing people to decipher your personal Rosetta stones is unprofessional and inconsiderate and can lead to disastrous misunderstandings.

HARD WORK

Not to be confused with long hours, hard work is what you have to do to succeed. Hard work involves planning and budgeting your time, organizing your activities, concentrating on what you are doing, and never being satisfied with less than your best. Working hard is working smart. Work hard for forty-five hours a week and you will outperform those who "put in" sixty hours a week.

HOTELS

Try to stay in the very best your expense account allows. The best ones are generally more comfortable and do more for your professional image.

HOUSEKEEPING

If you don't have someone to clean your house or apartment, invest the proceeds from your next raise and get someone to come in once or twice a week to do it. Your male co-workers don't have to work at two jobs. Why should you?

HUSBANDS

Supportive ones are the only kind that will do. Hassles at home can only make you less effective on the job. Your choice of a spouse makes a statement about your judgment in other areas. (The same goes for men, too.)

IDEAS

Dollars are the currency of U.S. business. Ideas are its wealth. Your ideas make you valuable to your company. Get them. Put your name on them. And make them happen.

IN-BOXES

Along with out-boxes, they belong on your secretary's desk, not on yours. If you need to separate incoming mail from outgoing mail, set aside two drawers in your desk for that purpose.

INTERVIEW (For jobs)

The interviewer wants to learn as much about you as possible. You want to put yourself in the most favorable light. It's a great battle of wits. Don't let the interviewer tip the scales by asking you to take psychological tests (unless you can censor the results) or by asking you illegal questions (e.g., marital status, family plans). By the same token, don't make yourself out to be something you are not. The company may end up buying something it later finds it has no need for. Interviewers like people with good manners, self-confidence, curiosity, enthusiasm, neatness, and intelligence.

LISTENING

The quintessential managerial skill. It leads to sensitivity and wisdom. It earns liking and respect.

LISTS

Many successful executives are compulsive list-makers. It's a good habit to form. Make daily lists of everything you have to do. And then make sure you do them. Lists are a good way to ensure that every important detail receives attention. They help keep you productive every minute of the day.

LONG HOURS

Except for a brief period for learning the ropes on a new job, don't work more than forty-five hours a week. If the job requires more than that, either the job is poorly defined or you are the wrong person for the job. Avoid working late. By going home when everyone else does, you signal that you are on top of things. If you must work overtime, come in early and spend the time *organizing* your activities for the rest of the day.

LUNCH

Lunch time is not free time. It is work time. Spend it with peers, subordinates, superiors, clients, customers, and other business associates. If you *must* order a drink (because everyone else is), stick to white wine. If everyone else is drinking martinis, order a very dry vermouth on the rocks with a twist. It looks like a martini, but you will be the only one at the table who can think straight for the rest of the day.

MAGAZINES

Subscribe to and read the following: *Time* or *Newsweek* for current events; *Sports Illustrated* so you won't be bored listening to the boys at lunch (but don't show off your knowledge of trivia); *Business Week* or *Forbes* for business news; and *Harvard Business Review* for articles of general management interest.

MARTHA

When Martha checked into the motel she discovered that someone in the corporate travel department had booked a single room to be shared with another company employee, Sam Wilson, with whom she was to work on the purchasing contract tomorrow. Sam, from the corporate legal department, was driving down from Cleveland and was scheduled to meet her at the motel later that evening. The reservation clerk insisted that all rooms in the good motels in town were booked up.

MATH

Avoid dumb statements such as "I have trouble balancing my checkbook." If you do, go to night school. A good command of algebra is essential for success in business; the calculus is desirable.

MBA DEGREE

If you don't have one, get one. Once you get one, your education hasn't stopped, it's just getting started. A good education merely teaches you what you *don't* know. Never volunteer that you have an MBA. Let your performance and behavior prompt people to ask.

*I disagree!
about getting one*

MEETINGS

Be sure you stay to the bitter end. Nothing happens until the last ten minutes when "consensus" is achieved. Be sure you understand what the "consensus" is.

MEMOS

Keep memo-writing to a minimum. People may forget what you say. They seldom forget what you put in writing. Above all, never write a memo while angry.

NAMES (Remembering)

Successful executives take an interest in the people they meet and concentrate on learning and remembering their names. If you have trouble remembering people's names, you are either not interested in them or not concentrating. Either way, you are in trouble. Work on it. When meeting someone for the first time, repeat the name back, even if it's hard to pronounce. Say, "Nice to meet you, Mr. Szyminski. Am I pronouncing your name correctly?"

NOTES

Written congratulations are a good idea. Send them to all business associates and co-workers who earn promotions, win recognition, or make job changes. Thank-you notes for special favors are also a good idea. So are phone calls for birthdays and company anniversary dates. These courtesies aren't feminine, they're professional.

NUMBERS

Data gain mystical precision once quantified. Don't be taken in just because something has a number tacked onto it. Garbage is still garbage, even after it's weighed.

ORGANIZING

Ninety per cent of your results come from activities that consume 10 per cent of your time. Make sure you know what those activities are. Do first those things that have to be done *now*. Do next those things that have to be done today. Don't worry today about things that don't have to be done until tomorrow. If they are really important enough to be done today, someone else will be doing them. If not, they can be left for tomorrow. If they still seem unimportant to you tomorrow, forget them. Either someone else will do them, or no one will do them, proving that they never needed to be done by you in the first place.

PATERNALISM

Although it takes a benign and often sincere form (he thinks he's doing you a favor), paternalism—keeping you from situations because you're a woman—is an insidious block to your personal development. When you see evidence of a paternalistic action, ask him: "What is it that I should avoid?"

PERFORMANCE APPRAISALS

This annual organizational ritual is almost universally performed badly. Nevertheless, insist on a thorough and candid appraisal of your performance by your boss at least once a year—and make sure it goes into your personnel folder. Try to get informal appraisals as often as possible. A good boss will do them without your asking. Do not confuse asking for an appraisal of your performance with asking for praise for your performance.

PLANNING

Measure twice, saw once. Time spent planning is time saved doing. The best guarantee that the job will get done the way you want it done is knowing in advance what you want to do and how and when you want to do it. Luck is the residue of design.

POLLY

Polly had barely sat down behind her new desk when Jack Reynolds introduced himself and requested her to see about a transfer for him. She recognized his name from her records as her district's top-volume salesman. When she asked why he wanted a transfer he replied, "I don't want to work for a woman."

PROBLEMS (Business)

Never go to your boss with your problems. Bosses have enough of their own. Go to them with solutions. Good managers love to talk about solutions. Say, "Here's the situation I'm in. Here are some options I've come up with. Could you help me think them through?"

PROBLEMS (Personal)

Don't bring them to the office. If they are serious enough to interfere with your work, tell your boss. Don't ask for advice, however. Real professionals won't give you any. They know they are neither psychiatrists nor priests.

PROTECTION

Keeping you from situations because you are a *woman* is paternalism. Keeping you from situations because you are a *human being* is not paternalism, it's protection. We all need protection from time to time. Sometimes your co-workers will protect you; sometimes your boss will protect you. It is, however, one of a mentor's prime functions.

PUBLIC SPEAKING

Supervisors speak in front of five people. Managers speak in front of twenty. Executives speak in front of hundreds. The CEO speaks on national TV. If public speaking makes you nervous, you have a problem. Act now. Take a course. Take every opportunity you can get to speak at meetings, conventions, anything. But get the nervousness out of your system. The more you delay, the worse it will be.

Robin — I took Dale Carnegie. It helped me immensely — our team how to speak to 200 families. ugh!

QUEEN BEES

Avoid them or you'll get stung. They come disguised as older female executives. They have made it. They don't give a damn about you. They are easy to spot. They collect drones.

QUESTIONS

More valuable than statements. Don't be afraid to ask them. Listen carefully to the answers. Make sure you understand them.

READING

Your brain needs care and feeding. Don't let your education go to waste. Read at least four books a month. A good mix is one classic, one best seller, one current topic, and one technical/business.

REASONS

In the old West, many gunfighters carried and used two guns, in case one misfired. When it's important for you to make your point, use two reasons, in case one misfires.

REPAIRMEN

Don't feel guilty if you have to take a couple of hours off to let the plumber in to repair your sink. Your boss takes time off for this kind of thing, too. Don't overdo it, however. It's easier to get a new sink than a new job.

SALARIES (Other people's)

Learn what your peers and bosses earn. Pay attention if a friend in Accounting wants to tell you. Let your male peers tell you at a three-martini (for them) lunch. This information is useful to you in many ways. It helps you determine how much of a raise to ask for. It tells you whether the company is serious about equal opportunity in general and your career in particular. It signals whether your boss's job is worth shooting for. If not, maybe you're working for the wrong organization.

SALARIES (Starting)

Try to avoid the "going rate." People who start at higher salaries tend to be more visible. It causes the boss to sweat and watch your every move (which is exactly what you want). And the company has a greater stake in seeing that you make it.

SECRETARIES

A good secretary, as any experienced manager knows, can double your effectiveness and triple your efficiency. Successful executives treat their secretaries with respect and consideration, thus earning their loyalty. You should do the same. Remember, she probably envies you. If you can serve as a role model for her and take an interest in her, her job, and her career, the envy will turn to admiration and you will have won her loyalty. Help her advance herself. Promote her if she deserves it. You will have lost a good secretary, but you may have gained a good friend.

SUBORDINATES

The easiest way to build an effective team is to make people proud to work for you. Set high standards. Treat people with respect. Show them how. Praise their efforts. Be unselfish: give, give, give. When your subordinates start to give back, give more.

SUBORDINATES (Male)

At first, most men won't like the idea of working for you. Simple reason, having little to do with you: they don't want to work for anybody, man or woman, who they think isn't going anywhere in the organization. You must prove to them that you are. When they see that you are, they will be eager to hitch their wagons to your star.

SURPRISES

Bosses are violently allergic to surprises. Never give your boss one. If things are turning sour, let your boss know before things begin to smell. Bosses are there to help.

TOKEN FEMALE

If holding the job you want involves being the token female, so what? Enjoy the visibility. Enjoy the challenge. Outperform all expectations. When you get promoted, they will probably hire another woman to take your place. And you won't be a token any more.

TRAVELING

Unless you are a born vagabond, traveling is a hassle. If you have to travel a lot, make things easy on yourself. Double-check all reservations and arrangements before you leave. Choose clothes that go together and won't wrinkle. Choose neutral shoes that match everything and are comfortable for walking. Choose a hair style that doesn't require curlers and a hair dryer. Buy small duplicate containers of your cosmetics and personal supplies so you are always ready to pack and go.

TREADING WATER

What you are doing when you get a 10 per cent raise. Six per cent is eaten up by inflation. The other 4 per cent is eaten up by your new (and higher) income tax bracket.

TYPEWRITERS

Unless your job involves writing, and typing is in your job description, don't have a typewriter in your office, no matter how convenient it would be. Typewriters are for secretaries. Let them do their thing. Your thing is managing.

VACATIONS

Take every day you've got coming to you. Same with holidays. Taking your vacation recharges your batteries, shows that you are on top of your job, and gives your co-workers a chance to see how much they miss not having you around.

WRITING

Precise language, well crafted, is a sign of a careful, intelligent, logical person. Most college graduates are illiterate. "If you don't write good, take a coarse."

ZEST

What you should bring to work with you in the morning. Also, what you should take home with you in the evening.